HOLT TRACTORS
PHOTO ARCHIVE

HOLT TRACTORS
PHOTO ARCHIVE
An Album of Steam and Early Gas Tractors

Photographs from the
Higgins Collection of the
Shields Library, University of California, Davis

Edited with introduction by
P. A. Letourneau

Iconografix
Photo Archive Series

Iconografix
P.O. Box 18433
Minneapolis, Minnesota 55418 USA

Library of Congress Card Number 93-80439
ISBN 1-882256-10-7

93 94 95 96 97 98 99 5 4 3 2 1

Cover and book design by Lou Gordon, Osceola, Wisconsin
Digital imaging by Pixelperfect, Madison, Wisconsin

Printed in the United States of America

PREFACE

The histories of machines and mechanical gadgets are contained in the books, journals, correspondence and personal papers stored in libraries and archives throughout the world. Written in tens of languages, covering thousands of subjects, the stories are recorded in millions of words.

Words are powerful. Yet, the impact of a single image, a photograph or an illustration, often relates more than dozens of pages of text. Fortunately, many of the libraries and archives that house the words also preserve the images.

In the Photo Archive Series, Iconografix reproduces photographs and illustrations selected from public and private collections. The images are chosen to tell a story...to capture the character of their subject. Reproduced as found, they are accompanied by the captions made available by the archive.

The Iconografix Photo Archive Series is dedicated to young and old alike, the enthusiast, the collector and anyone who, like us, is fascinated by "things" mechanical.

ACKNOWLEDGMENTS

Most of the photographs appearing in this book were selected from an album compiled by Holt Manufacturing Company. The album is part of the Higgins Collection, Shields Library, Special Collections, University of California, Davis. We reproduce the photographs with their permission. We appreciate their cooperation, and particularly wish to thank John Skarstad, Curator Special Collections, for his assistance and enthusiasm for this project.

The Caterpillar Inc. Corporate Archives kindly provided supplemental photographs (pages 11, 18, 19, 23, 27, 51, 70, and 71) and reference materials. We thank Joyce Luster, Corporate Archivist.

We are most grateful to Lorry Dunning for his research into the history of the particular machines featured in this book. Virtually no information regarding the machines accompanied the photographs. Mr. Dunning's work made writing captions for the photographs possible. Armed with his knowledge of Holt equipment, and after reviewing serial number and production records, Mr. Dunning was able to determine model designations for most of the machines.

For certain sales and shipment details, dates of production, and individual specifications, Mr. Dunning consulted the Holt Manufacturing Company Production Record Book, 1894-1912. A part of the Holt Industrial Archives, it is preserved at The Haggin Museum, Stockton, California. We thank The Haggin Museum for permission to reproduce this information.

Benjamin Holt, father of the Caterpillar tractor, co-founder of Holt Manufacturing Company and its president until his death in 1920.

INTRODUCTION

Holt Manufacturing Company was incorporated in 1892, as the successor to the Stockton Wheel Company, Stockton, California. Organized in 1883, Stockton Wheel Company built its first combined harvester in 1886. Under the leadership and genius of Benjamin Holt, the company soon became the Western United States' leading combine manufacturer.

While teams of horses or mules were commonly used to pull combines of this era, the tireless steam traction engine proved both more reliable and more efficient. Holt's position as a combine manufacturer undoubtedly led to its entry into the steam traction market. "Betsy," Benjamin Holt's first steam traction engine, was built in 1890. It featured a single 10.25 x 12-inch cylinder and a round "Scotch marine" boiler. Like Holt combines, it was driven by heavy link chains and sprockets, rather than gears. Subsequent production tractors employed a single 10.25 x 12-inch, 10.5 x 12-inch, or 11 x 12-inch steam cylinder, rated from 40 to 70 horsepower.

Holt built 133 steam traction engines, over a period of twenty years. Most were sold to farming operations for use in plowing, planting, and harvesting, and to freighting, logging, and mining operations for use in transporting materials. As can be seen in the photographs, the configurations of the tractors varied as to the positions of boilers, flywheels, drive chains, smoke stacks, and water tanks, as well as in the size and types of drive wheels employed. While Holt production records remain intact, there is little information available regarding these design differences. It would appear that Benjamin Holt continually worked at the design and construction of these machines and, to varying degrees, each was unique.

It is particularly interesting to note the width of wheels fitted to the traction engines photographed at work in farm fields. Many were fitted with extra-wide drive wheels and sets of auxiliary wheels that prevented these heavy tractors from sinking to their axles in soft, soggy, or sandy soils. Such machines were, of course, even heavier and more difficult to maneuver. It was the realization that increasingly wider conventional wheels were not an adequate means to improve tractor flotation or traction that inspired Benjamin Holt to develop his concept of the track machine.

In late 1904, Holt began experiments with track machines. A number of prototypes were built, before a track-equipped steamer was sold in December 1906. The idea of tracks, or "platform wheels" as they were also known, was a good one. However, steam machines were heavy, crude, and expensive to operate. Horses were still required to carry water and fuel to tractors in the field. Benjamin Holt recognized that the gasoline engine offered a more efficient means of power, and one by which the weight of the tractor could also be reduced.

Even as the first steam Caterpillars were being built, Holt began experiments with gas engine-powered machines. A separate company, Aurora Engine Company, was organized to build gas engines, and the first gas engine Caterpillar, No. 1001, was built in the fall of 1906. Over a year of testing followed, before No. 1002 was built in 1908. Two additional gas tractors were built in 1908 and were the first units sold: one for farm use; the other to the city of Los Angeles, the first of 28 gas Caterpillars purchased for work on construction of the Los Angeles Aqueduct. Sales of machines grew rapidly, and by 1910 Holt opened its Peoria, Illinois factory to supply the growing demand of the Midwest and Eastern U.S. markets. By 1912, approximately 760 gas tractors had been sold.

With one exception of a tractor built in Peoria, the gas Caterpillars featured in this book were built in Stockton between 1908 and 1912. Holt production records generally made no reference to model designations. Rather, they reported engine size and, in some cases, a horsepower rating. Subsequent serial number lists identify models of this period as the Models 40, 40-45, 45, and 60. Using both production records and serial number lists, we have identified and labelled most of the machines with model designation.

While model designations are assumed to correspond to brake horsepower ratings, it is not certain that the early Holt 40s, indeed, generated 40 brake horsepower. For early production units, there is evidence that suggests its 4-cylinder engine with 6 x 8-inch bore and stroke developed only 25 to 30 horsepower. To confuse matters more, the Model 40-45, a series of as few as 40 tractors built only in Stockton, appear identical to the Model 40. Production records indicate, however, that they were fitted with a larger 6.5 x 8-inch engine rated at 45 brake horsepower. This same 6.5 x 8-inch engine was fitted to all Holt 45s. A 7 x 8-inch 4-cylinder engine was fitted to the Holt 60.

Reports of the performance of machines that worked on the Los Angeles Aqueduct project indicated a number of weaknesses existed in these early Holt 40s. Engineering changes were made to virtually every component that resulted in significant improvements. While such changes are difficult to distinguish in the photos in this book, there are some obvious changes to note. For example, early Holt 40s featured five track rollers per track and chain link steering. Later Holt 40s, as well as 45s and 60s, featured four track rollers and worm and gear steering. Further differences in the weight of the main frames, gearing, radiators, engine exhausts, cooling fans, and fuel tanks should also be noted for all models.

This book is the most complete collection of photographs of either Holt steamers or early Caterpillar tractors yet published. It will prove valuable and fascinating to every Holt and Caterpillar tractor enthusiast.

The Holt factory, Stockton, California, as it appeared in 1889.

Interior views of the Stockton factory.

Holt workers, circa World War I.

STEAM TRACTORS

A Holt steam traction engine and a road locomotive. Note the directional arrow mounted to the front wheel.

Holt records identified tractors by serial number and the size of the steam cylinder. Model designations were not used. Engine No. 26 was built in 1900.

Holt sold many tractors for use as freighting engines. This tractor is pulling six wagons of lumber from a California mill.

Engine No. 37 was equipped with a single 11 x 12-inch steam cylinder rated at 60 to 65 horsepower. Photographed at work in San Francisco.

20

Sold by Pliny Holt, Benjamin's nephew, No. 37 was delivered to Union Traction Company in February 1900.

Engine No. 44, equipped with a single 11 x 12-inch cylinder, was sold to Copper King Limited, San Francisco, in December 1901.

No. 51, one of fifteen engines built in 1902, featured hydraulic steering. The steering cylinder operated on pressurized hot water.

No. 60 featured a single 10.5 x 12-inch steam cylinder rated at 50 horsepower.

No. 66 was shipped to Standard Lumber Company, Deer Park, Washington, in December 1902.

Built in 1904, No. 77 was later converted to a track machine (see page 63).

No. 83 featured an 11 x 12-inch cylinder and 42 x 74-inch drive wheels. Sold by Pliny Holt in 1905, it was shipped to Mesa, Arizona.

No. 95, with 11 x 12-inch cylinder and 24-inch wide wheels, was sold by Pliny Holt and shipped to Mountain Transportation Company in November 1905. Note headlight.

No. 119, sold by Pliny Holt to Compania Metalurgica y Refinadora Del Pacifica, was one of three engines shipped to Sonora, Mexico in August 1907.

Rear view of No. 119. The steam cylinder measured 11 x 12-inches. The rear wheels measured 24 x 90-inches.

Steam traction engine No. 96 was built in 1905.

A Holt steam traction engine freighting outfit.

No. 55, equipped with 11 x 12-inch cylinder and 24 x 78-inch wheels, pulling logging wagons.

No. 36 was sold to Holt Freight Co., Stockton, and shipped to Anderson, California in June 1902.

Freighting lumber from a California mill.

Freighting wagons with a Holt steam traction engine, circa 1906.

No. 92 pulling four ore wagons, circa 1906.

No. 92, equipped with 11 x 12-inch cylinder and 24 x 78-inch wheels, was sold to Chewelah Copper King Mining Co. in April 1905.

No. 92 pulling four ore wagons, circa 1906.

No. 20 with auxiliary rear wheels and front wooden barrel wheel that prevented the tractor from sinking into the soft soil of the San Joaquin River Valley.

A Holt steam traction engine with auxiliary steam engine that supplied added horsepower.

Holt steam traction engine pulling harrows. The tractor was fitted with optional 42-inch wide drive wheels and 42-inch auxiliary wheels.

Holt steam traction engine pulling three disc harrows.

An 1897 photo of a Holt outfit plowing, seeding and harrowing a strip 44 feet wide.

Legend has it that each wheel of this giant measured 72 inches wide.

Side and rear views of a Holt steamer fitted with 42-inch drive and auxiliary wheels.

A view of the front tiller wheel and its chain link steering.

Spark arresters were commonly fitted during the dry harvest season. Note the sacks of grain carried on the platform.

Rear view of a Holt combine with extended header.

Holt steamer and Holt Standard Double Drive Combine. In 1900, Holt offered outfits such as this for $7,000.

A Holt steamer and combine with its crew. Seven to eight man crews were commonly required to manage the tractor and harvester.

A Holt steam traction engine drawing water for its boiler.

No. 77, converted from a wheel to a track-type tractor, became a prototype used to test the Caterpillar principle.

An early steam Caterpillar with 9-foot track. The track shoes were made of wooden slats.

A rear view showing Holt's simple but ingenious chain drive system.

No. 122, featured a 10.25 x 12-inch cylinder and 30-inch wide track. Sold secondhand in February 1910, there is no record of its original sale.

GASOLINE TRACTORS

Two views of an early Holt gas tractor prototype.

The tractor incorporated Holt steam traction engine components with a gasoline engine purchased from an outside source.

The Aurora engine used in the first Holt gasoline Caterpillar, built in 1906. The 4-cylinder engine featured 6 x 8-inch bore and stroke.

A test of No. 1002, the second gas Caterpillar tractor, built in 1908. Note that early units featured five track rollers.

Two Model 40s loaded for shipment to Sacramento Valley Sugar Co., Hamilton City, California. 1909.

No. 1105, a Model 45, was delivered June 1910 to the C. Parker Holt Ranch. The engine, rated at 45 brake horsepower, featured 6.5 x 8-inch bore and stroke.

No. 1057, a Model 40-45, featured 3-speeds and frame and steering improvements introduced in 1910.

Sold in August 1909, No. 1057 was shipped to Frank H. Kay, Tolo, Oregon. Four track rollers were used per track, instead of five.

No. 1178, a 1910 special wide-tread Model 45, featured improved steering, wood rim steering wheel, cloth top, four rollers, and 6.5 x 8-inch engine.

No. 1178 was sold to Charles Morling of Stockton, California.

No. 1003, the first Caterpillar gas tractor sold.

No. 1003, a Model 40, first of 28 Caterpillars sold to the city of Los Angeles between 1908 and 1910.

No. 1164, a Model 45, featured a 45 horsepower, 6.5 x 8-inch engine. Note four track rollers, 6-bladed fan, and front steering gears in place of earlier chain link mechanism.

No. 1164 was sold November 1910 to the Nevada Wonder Mining Co., Compton, California.

Two views of a Model 40 built prior to 1910.

No. 1226, a Model 60, was one of ten Caterpillars shipped to Argentina in 1911. The Holt 60 featured a 7 x 8-inch, 4-cylinder engine rated at 60 brake horsepower.

No. 1226, built in Stockton, featured a belt pulley, corrugated tin roof, and 4-roller track. The 60 was also built in Peoria.

Two views of a Model 40 built in Peoria around 1913. Note the corrugated roof, 4-roller track, rear spool, and placement of the radiator in front of the engine fan.

This tractor bore the Holt Caterpillar Co. name, the registered name of the Peoria operation begun in 1909.

Rear view of a Model 45 built in 1910 or 1911.

Rear view of a Model 60 built in Stockton. Note the belt pulley.

A Model 40-45, with one set of tracks and one wheel, equipped as a road grader.

This machine, less the grader blade, may have been the 1909 prototype Benjamin Holt purportedly designed for use in orchards.

No. 1193, a Holt 45, with 6.5 x 8-inch engine, 24-inch tread, 4-roller track, and cloth top. It was sold January 1911 to Lynch & Woods, Stockton, California.

No. 1055, a 1909 Model 40, one of three such tractors sold to American Beet Sugar Company, Oxnard, California.

A Model 40 built in Stockton in 1908 or 1909. The chain link steering, lighter frame, and 5-roller track indicate it was an early unit.

A Model 60 built in Stockton between 1911 and 1913. Note the extended track pads.

A Model 60 with belt pulley, built in Stockton between 1911 and 1913.

An early Model 40.

No. 1013 was one of 53 Holt 40s built in 1909. Sold by Holt's Walla Walla branch, it was shipped to Witherow, Washington.

A rare Holt 60 wheel tractor equipped with a 60 horsepower, 4-cylinder engine of 7 x 8-inch bore and stroke.

Listed in production records as a "1911 Gasoline Round-Wheel Caterpillar," this was the only such tractor built in Stockton.

The tiller wheel removed on a Model 40-45 demonstrated the tractor's balance.

A Model 40-45 pumping water for irrigation. Lovelock, Nevada. 1910.

A 1908 or 1909 Model 40 (possibly No. 1003) and Holt side-dump ore wagon working on the Los Angeles Aqueduct project.

Over 80 Holt ore wagons were used on the L. A. Aqueduct project.

A Holt Model 40, one of six freighting outfits operated by Producers Transportation Company, at work hauling oil.

The L. A. Aqueduct was a major test of the early Caterpillar. A final review indicated horses did the job for one-half the cost.

Hauling heavy loads of material for the L. A. Aqueduct took its toll of engines, clutches and transmissions.

Most of the Caterpillars on the project were eventually abandoned. Some were sold to local farmers.

No. 1200, a Holt 45, and its load in front of the Stockton factory.

Holt 45 fitted with an acetylene headlight.

Caterpillar No. 1001 or 1002 pulling wagons in a circle.

A train of 19 Holt wagons ready for shipment. 1910.

Two Model 40s freighting construction materials across the Mojave Desert.

Breaking virgin sod, with eight 14-inch plow bottoms. Dunkirk, Montana. 1910.

A 1909 Holt 40 in a field test near the Stockton factory.

Caterpillar pulling 160 inches of plows. Williams, California. 1910.

Model 40-45 turning salt grass sod with a Haines plow. Grizzly Island, Suisun, California. 1910.

Model 40, Serial No. 1003, in a field test before its sale to the city of Los Angeles.

124

Holt Model 40, Serial No. 1012, plowing.

No. 1012 was shipped to Holt's Walla Walla branch in May 1909.

An early Model 40 pulling nine 14-inch plow bottoms. The owner plowed an average 30 acres per day on his 960 acre Oregon farm.

The first gas Caterpillar, No. 1001, and a Holt harvester. Built in 1906, this tractor was extensively tested before No. 1002 was built in 1908.

Opposite views of a 1910 Model 45, Serial No. 1105, and a Holt harvester.

Operating on the C. Parker Holt Ranch, No. 1105 cut, threshed, and sacked 1126 sacks of barley in one day.

A Holt 40-45, with roller, breaking tule jungle. Alpaugh, California. 1910.

A modified Holt 40-45, with one track and one wheel, pulling a flat wagon loaded with hay.

A Holt tank wagon. Holt built a wide-ranging line of carts, wagons, and tanks.

A Holt 8-ton ore wagon, with 4 cubic yard capacity, weighed approximately 6450 pounds. Front wheels measured 12 x 48-inches. Rear wheels measured 12 x 64-inches.

Holt horse-drawn dump cart.

A Holt flat wagon filled with wood.

The Iconografix Photo Archive Series includes:

JOHN DEERE MODEL D Photo Archive	ISBN 1-882256-00-X
JOHN DEERE MODEL B Photo Archive	ISBN 1-882256-01-8
FARMALL F-SERIES Photo Archive	ISBN 1-882256-02-6
FARMALL MODEL H Photo Archive	ISBN 1-882256-03-4
CATERPILLAR THIRTY Photo Archive	ISBN 1-882256-04-2
CATERPILLAR SIXTY Photo Archive	ISBN 1-882256-05-0
TWIN CITY TRACTOR Photo Archive	ISBN 1-882256-06-9
MINNEAPOLIS-MOLINE U-SERIES Photo Archive	ISBN 1-882256-07-7
HART-PARR Photo Archive	ISBN 1-882256-08-5
OLIVER TRACTOR Photo Archive	ISBN 1-882256-09-3
HOLT TRACTORS Photo Archive	ISBN 1-882256-10-7
RUSSELL GRADERS Photo Archive	ISBN 1-882256-11-5

The Iconografix Photo Archive Series is available from direct mail specialty book dealers and bookstores throughout the world, or can be ordered from the publisher.

For information write to:

Iconografix
P.O. Box 609   or
Osceola, Wisconsin 54020

Telephone: (715) 294-2792
(800) 289-3504 (US and Canada only)
Fax: (715) 294-3414